HOWARD HUGE

HOWARD HUGE

by Bill Hoest

LYLE STUART INC.
Secaucus, New Jersey

First edition

Queries regarding rights and permissions
should be address to:
Lyle Stuart Inc.
120 Enterprise Ave., Secaucus, N.J. 07094

Published by Lyle Stuart Inc.
Published simultaneously in Canada by
Musson Book Company
A division of General Publishing Co. Limited
Don Mills, Ontario.

Manufactured in the United States of America.

Library of Congress Cataloging in Publications Data

Hoest, Bill.
    Howard Huge

    1. American wit and humor, Pictorial.   I. Title.
NC1429.H542A4   1981   741.5'973   81-16736
ISBN 0-8184-0321-7   AACR2

FOREWORD
by Walter Anderson
Editor of *Parade* Magazine

Editors depend on other people for their successes, because any good magazine represents a staff rather than a solo effort. Assembling the staff, selecting the individual writers, artists and other contributors—that's the real trick. And in few instances have I been more content and gratified with a selection that I've made for *Parade* magazine than Bill Hoest, the creator of Howard Huge, the affable animal whose adventures are so delightfully depicted in the pages of this book.

Howard is like no dog I've ever met, and Bill, his best friend, is like no other cartoonist. In fact, I don't know if cartoonist—as honorable a term as it is—is an adequate word for Bill. He's an artist, a humorist and a wonderful human being all combined into one. You don't meet a Bill Hoest every day, any more than you meet a Howard Huge.

We're proud to have him in the pages of *Parade*, and we hope he will find some additional friends and admirers within the covers of this book. Howard Huge is strictly Bill Hoest's creation, but I'm very pleased to have had my share in helping introduce him to so many friends throughout the country. Shake hands, Howard.

"I don't have a big brother to look up to—I have Howard."

"Teaching Howard to do tricks is okay,
but next time get a bigger hoop."

"Yes, a lot of kids at camp were homesick—those with dogs."

"Let me know if his looking over your shoulder bothers you."

"His real name is Howard Huge,
but if you have something to
eat, he'll answer to anything."

"He's a great watchdog. He watches Dallas, Three's Company, and Odd Couple reruns."

"Howard, sit!"

"Good dog."

②

"We'll be right back, Howard. Are you going to act like a little puppy the rest of your life?"

"Forgive me for not getting up."

"Howard! I've told you
not to play in the street!"

"I figured out that thirty-three times around Howard
is a quarter of a mile."

DEAR HOWARD......

Dear Howard,
I bury a lot of bones, but then I can't remember where I've buried them. What can I do?...Forgetful Foxhound

Dear Forgetful,
What really helped me was the memory course I took six months ago or maybe it was a year ago. I went every Wednesday or Thursday for either six or eight weeks. It changed my life.

Dear Howard,
I'm a 115 pound, attack-trained Doberman. Where can I sleep?...Pooped Pinscher

Dear Pooped,
Anyplace you want to.

Dear Howard,
My human does a lot of things wrong. What should I do?...Smart Saluki

Dear Smart,
Hit him on the head with a rolled-up newspaper.

"Wow! Everything he eats must turn to dog!"

"You should have seen him <u>before</u> we gave him pep pills!"

"Why wasn't he invited to the wedding? He's family."

"I liked him better as a puppy."

"They put him in
the underachievers' class."

"Why can't you train him to scratch at the door like other dogs?"

"There's only one way to get him off the sofa—
go open the refrigerator door."

"Goodbye, Howard.
Good luck, sir."

"It's no use, Louie....
I'll just have to wait until he wakes up!"

"You know that's not the stick I threw!"

"Of course I love him. If I didn't, I couldn't stand him!"

"It was the only way I could get him to go for a walk."

"Big is too better!"

"Look, Mom—Howard's dreaming he's being brave."

"Give him a bath? Wouldn't it be easier just to run him through the car wash?"

"I'm sorry. I can't stop him from wagging his tail.
He's just friendly."

"It's your own fault
for sitting in his chair."

"Now, remember, Howard—
technically I'm your master."

"I'm planting. He's unplanting."

"He scratches himself 'cause he's
the only one who knows where it itches."

"They got my wallet
and his flea collar."

"If you won't chase him,
at least get your own chair."

"No, he doesn't bite…but you have to watch out for his terrible bark."

"Honey, what happened? The punch is all gone!"

DEAR HOWARD......

Dear Howard,
The mailman arrives about four-thirty every day, and I go after him. Is that all right?...Shy Shepherd

Dear Shy,
Yessir...nothing like a little nip before dinner.

Dear Howard,
I lost my flea collar. What should I do?...Uncollared Collie

Dear Uncollared,
Scratch.

Dear Howard,
I like cats. Is that okay?...Concerned Corgi

Dear Concerned,
Sure. As long as you're both consenting adults.

"Hey, Dad, come over here in the shade!"

"Isn't that cute? He wants you to take him for a ride!"

"You stay here, Howard. I have to go out with my second-best friend."

"He <u>is</u> sitting down."

"You give him a ticket."

"I got a shockproof, waterproof, antimagnetic, indestructible watch for my birthday and he ate it!"

"See what happens when you pull on your leash?"

"Stop dreaming, Howard."

"Sure he's wagging his tail. That's not the end I'm worried about."

"It's okay, Dad. Howard's trying to speed up the mails."

"Don't worry, Mom. Maybe next year they'll have a 'clumsy' category!"

"Let me guess....It's a sweater for Howard for Christmas."

DEAR HOWARD......

Dear Howard,
My owner recently bought a cat. He's a nice guy, but all he says is, "Meow." What can I do?...Bored Basset

Dear Bored,
Learn to say, "Meow." A second language can come in handy.

Dear Howard,
What's the most popular name for a dog; "Rover," "Fido," or "Spot"?...Wondering Weimaraner

Dear Wondering,
"Down, Boy."

Dear Howard,
I have taught my human being to give me dog biscuits whenever I sit up, and to throw sticks so I can chase them, and he's very cute when he does it. Lately, however, he's started acting like the whole thing was his idea and he's taking credit for everything. What should I do?...Puzzled Pointer

Dear Puzzled,
Humor him. It will increase his sense of self-importance and probably even his performance.

HOWARD HUGE FRIENDS

"You forgot to let the dog back in."

"Let him loose, Harry. They're only bills."

"Don't pay any attention to him. He just gets a
little annoyed when people continually interrupt me."

"Isn't that cute. He's trying to tell us something."

"If the pep pills don't work, you can always use him as a rug."

"No, no. I Don't dare give you any of this. You'd never forgive me."

"Now what have you been up to?"

"Can't he play a tune the dog doesn't know?"

"They say she's an only dog."

"Yes, I know the newspaper is out there. What I want you to do is fetch it!"

"Watch how I've got him trained. When I bring the stick to him he knows how to throw it out again."

"...And a ball, a rubber bone, a new leash, a dish with my name on it..."

"Did you put your sports car in his doghouse again?"

"My sister couldn't come, so
I brought Howard instead."

"Howard! Put that back where you found it!"

"He's right, you know. You forgot his supper again."

"The dog's okay, but watch out for that kid."

"It's hard to believe there was room for two of him on the ark."

"<u>You</u> tell him he's out."

"Don't take Howard too far, now!"

"Oh…am I in your chair?"

"No, no, Howard! Just the paper!"

"On second thought, let's give him a nice bone and let him go with a warning."

"Why do I have to take a bath anyway? Howard <u>likes</u> the way I smell!"

DEAR HOWARD......

Dear Howard,
Do you think a dog will become President of the United States?...Political Poodle

Dear Political,
No, I think most dogs have too much sense.

Dear Howard,
Is it true you can't teach an old dog new tricks?...Aging Afghan

Dear Aging,
Absolutely not. That saying was made up by an old dog who didn't want to be bothered.

Dear Howard,
My master won't let me beg at the table for scraps. What should I do?...Begging Beagle

Dear Begging,
I don't know, but stay off the corner of Elm and Third.

"Sure he can do tricks. When he sees me he wags his tail."

"He just learned how
to ring the doorbell."

"No, it's not an earthquake, Mother. It's just Howard scratching himself."

"He brought you the paper...the least you could do is read the comics to him!"

"Honey, tell him this is Saturday!
I won't be late for work!"

"It's a secret, Dad. Don't tell Howard that Jennifer is on his back."

"No, He's not chasing a cat. A cat is chasing <u>him</u>!"

"If Howard bothers you, just ignore him!"

"He got too big for the car, so we got a station wagon.
 He got too big for the station wagon, so…"

"It's not that I begrudge him the food...
it's just that I can't deduct him as a dependent!"

"Watch out for him, Howard—he bites."

"Lassie would go for help."

"I think he's putting in a basement."

DEAR HOWARD......

Dear Howard,
I'm a little too young for a doghouse. Where should I sleep?...Young Yorkie

Dear Young,
Try a pup tent.

Dear Howard,
What do you put on your dog food to keep it so moist?...Dry-Mouthed Dachshund

Dear Dry-Mouthed,
I use a T-bone steak.

Dear Howard,
What is the best way to punish your master?...Revengeful Retriever

Dear Revengeful,
Next Sunday morning, steal one of his golf clubs and hide it in his church.

"That's quite a school. Tomorrow they want him to bring in a pocket calculator."

"He's not too proud to beg, Dad—he's too lazy."

"He feels that nobody notices him."

"Don't call him. I'm pressing flowers in some books."

"When we first got him
   you thought he was cuddly, remember?"

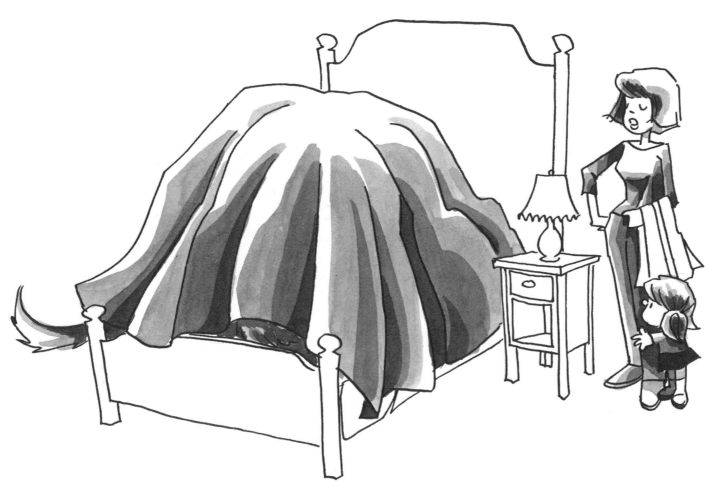

"Come out, Howard. I know you're in there."

"Frankly, I felt safer when we had burglars!"

"He ate another BEWARE OF DOG sign."

"Howard scratched himself on a cat."

"Howard! Time for your afternoon snack!"

"Honey, you have to do something! The dog catcher locked
Howard in his truck and took him to the pound!"

"Yes, he can do tricks! He can make twenty dollars' worth of chopped meat disappear just like that!"

"I taught him to roll over and play dead.
Now I have to teach him to come back to life."

DEAR HOWARD......

Dear Howard,
I've learned to roll over, sit up, and play dead. Do you think I should pursue a career in the theatre?...Theatrical Terrier

Dear Theatrical,
I'd suggest you try a little summer stock first.

Dear Howard,
Any suggestions on how I can stop chasing postmen?...Chasing Chihuahua

Dear Chasing,
Keep it up. Anything to speed up the mail.

Dear Howard,
How can you make your human come to you when you call him?...Sputtering Spitz

Dear Sputtering,
Pretend you've had an accident on the rug.

"Sugar is an economy-class model."

"If I can arrange for a nap time,
will you go to obedience school?"

"Well, to make a long story short…"

"No one will ever believe that all we did was try to give Howard a bath."

"I bought six books on dog training. He ate every one."

"Sorry, Howard...you know what the vet said—
only one bag a day."

"Howard's washing and we're drying."

"Honey, can I speak to you...alone?"

"Don't say anything. Howard thinks he's in disguise."

"Howard's no watch dog, but he knows 'sit.'"

"I'm wondering if you have anything for a dog who doesn't like exercise and doesn't care how he looks or smells."

"Look, you're no pretty picture when you get up in the morning, either!"

DEAR HOWARD......

Dear Howard,
What do you think of flea collars?...
Chic Shnauzer

Dear Chic,
Well, if the fleas want to wear them it's all right with me.

Dear Howard,
My owner is trying to teach me a lot of new tricks. How can I convince him that I'm an old dog?...Drooping Dalmation

Dear Drooping,
Don't learn any.

Dear Howard,
My master is trying to paper train me on a paper with your column in it. What should I do?...Pondering Pekinese

Dear Pondering,
Use his pants leg.

The Story of Howard Huge

HOWARD HUGE was not a planned dog...he was an accident.

The family was looking for a Labrador Retriever as a companion to an aging, ladylike black Lab. The kennel was vibrant with lively Labrador puppies. Alone, in a too-small cage, was a furry and silent little animal. Unable to stand, he was placidly eyeing the pre-Christmas shoppers from his prone position.

The family opened the too-small cage and took the disheveled furry dog out for a stretch. He tried his paws and immediately sprawled on his belly. Happily he lay there, his disposition unruffled.

To the sharp questioning by the family, the kennel owner answered that the breeder in Minnesota had shipped the dog east two weeks before and that his growth had been so swift that he had outgrown the cage. He also speculated that the dog had been sent to the wrong kennel (where he remained unwanted) and had been taken from his mother too soon in the breeder's haste to "catch" the Christmas buyers. The family was appalled.

With something less than enthusiasm, the family kept looking at the playful Labrador puppies. But the littlest girl held the disheveled dog on her shoulder, where he promptly fell asleep. Without being able to come to a decision, the family started to leave and told the littlest girl to put the disheveled dog back. His too-big paws caught on her sweater as she returned him to his too-small cage. The good-natured animal kissed her face and lay quietly alone. The family was captivated. Their education began.

This furry, disheveled, good-natured, placid puppy was a Saint Bernard. He would eventually become an enormous, clumsy, comic, loyal and lovable member of the family and share over thirteen hilarious years with them. HOWARD HUGE is the immortalization of that gentle giant.